Contents

*Possible science fair experiments

BIOLOGY

MOTION, WEIGHT, & BALANCE

CRYSTALS, CLEANING, & WATER

*Possible science fair experiments

AIR & GASES

Dedication

For Dianne, who has always been there

Acknowledgments

My family has been very helpful with parts of this book, especially in tolerating my impatience and mood swings. My wife, Dianne, did a little of everything. My son Shane Meador provided the illustrations, my daughter Cassie Meador and my son Joshua Wellnitz served as models for the photographs. Thanks, gang! Additional thanks goes to Valerie Spratlin for the photographs and to Kim Tabor and April Nolan of TAB Books for suggestions.

Notes to children

I wrote this book so you could have fun with science. Your kitchen or yard can become your own science laboratory. You don't need fancy equipment. Almost everything you need should be found in your home.

Many of the experiments will surprise you. They might seem like magic, and you can amaze your friends with "tricks." But the experiments are not magic: They all are based on the rules of science.

Look through the book and find one or two experiments you find interesting. (Each experiment tells you at the beginning what happens.) Gather all the materials you will need for the experiment, and keep the materials in one place.

Before beginning, be sure to read the section, *Symbols Used in This Book*. Become familiar with the meanings of the symbols. They provide you with all the safety precautions you should practice. Pay special attention to whether you should have an adult present when you do the experiment. Always keep safety in mind when doing any science experiment.

When you are ready to start an experiment, first read the procedure, but do not read the explanation until you have done the experiment. Then complete the experiment, following the directions exactly as they are written. Look at the pictures to be sure you have set things up correctly.

Use all of your senses as you observe what happens. If you must write something down, such as a measurement, do it as soon as you make the measurement. Your memory is often not as good as it seems.

Try to explain what happened and why. You might want to repeat the experiment one or two more times. Now look at the explanation to see if you figured it out. Try to talk about the experiment with an adult.

After you have done the experiment, try changing some of the materials and experiment on your own. Be curious! Have fun! Be safe!

If you have questions or did some new and interesting things, or would just like to comment on the book, please write to me:

Dr. Bill Wellnitz
Biology Department
Augusta College
Augusta, Georgia 30910

Notes to adults

This book, like its predecessors, had its origin with my children. Many times when they had friends over, rather than making cookies, we would do science experiments in the kitchen. Our kitchen became a wonderful laboratory, and soon the number of children wanting to do kitchen science exceeded the space of our kitchen. The demand for science experiments and experience quickly grew into three different, weekend science classes for children at Augusta College.

The intent of this book is threefold:

1. To expose children to principles and procedures of science
2. To show children that science is, and can be, fun
3. To stimulate thinking and creativity

By showing young children that science is fun, I hope to encourage them to maintain an interest in and an appreciation for science.

Understanding scientific concepts requires active participation, but it is not necessary to use sophisticated equipment. Stimulating creative thinking often involves exposure to a discrepant, or surprising, event. Convincing children that science is fun demands that they be allowed to play and experiment on their own.

Consequently, the simple, safe experiments in this book:

- Use items that are readily available in the home
- Often appear as magic tricks
- Are open-ended

All experiments have been "kid-tested" many times, and most require less than 30 minutes to complete.

Although most experiments can be done by children alone, I encourage you to become involved—but only as a guide. Some experiments demand your assistance and should not be done by children alone. These experiments require the use of a stove, flames, or electricity; such experiments are clearly indicated by the icons at the start of each experiment.

Help the children find the materials they will need, but let them do the experiment themselves. Discuss the results with them, and encourage them to think of explanations and other uses of the process involved.

Two important aspects of science are observation and measurement. Encourage your children to use all their senses, to measure accurately, and to record their observations. For some experiments, I have provided graphs to show children how to present results.

Many of the experiments are intentionally open-ended. Children are naturally curious and will want to vary the procedure or try different materials. Don't become alarmed if they do this; just make certain they do the experiment as written on their first attempt. Many a great discovery has come from someone modifying an existing procedure.

Each of the seven parts in the book begins with a brief description of the area of science the children will explore through completing the experiments that follow. Also included in this introductory material is a list of "important words," the definitions of which can all be found in the glossary. Encourage the children to learn these words and to expand their scientific vocabulary.

The experiments in this book provide a solid background in scientific principles and methodology and the techniques can easily be applied to other situations. Some of the experiments, with expansion and modification, could easily become science fair projects. While my intent is not to provide a listing of science fair projects, those experiments that would make good potential science fair projects are indicated by * in the table of contents. If your child does a science fair project, be sure that he or she actually does the work.

Finally, you might find you enjoy many of the experiments; and if you have a fear of science, you, too, may discover that science can be fun. I welcome your comments, both positive and negative; my address appears in *Notes to Children*.

Symbols used in this book

adult supervision

fire

electricity

scissors

sharp object

stove

safety goggles

dangerous chemical

Part 1
Goo, glue, & floppy things

This section contains experiments that deal with different chemicals. You will see that certain chemicals cause other chemicals to change. Some of these changes have the effect of breaking or dissolving the structure made by the chemical. Other changes cause *molecules* to be hooked together to make new and different structures. Some of the things that you will make are difficult to describe because they behave both like liquids and solids.

important words

☆ curd
☆ gravity
☆ mineral
☆ molecule
☆ precipitate

1
The floppy bone

objective ☆ Everyone knows that bones are hard and stiff. You can make a bone that will easily bend. *Note:* This experiment will take 1 to 2 weeks.

materials ☆
- ☐ leg or wing bone from piece of chicken
- ☐ tall glass or jar
- ☐ 2 or 3 bottles of vinegar

procedure ☆ 1. Remove as much meat as possible from the bone. Place the bone in the jar.

Soak the bone in vinegar.

2. Pour the vinegar into the jar so that the bone is covered.
3. Change the vinegar in the jar every 3 days.
4. After 1 or 2 weeks, remove the bone from the vinegar. It will be floppy, not stiff.

explanation ☆ A *mineral* (a natural substance made up of one type of molecule) in the bones makes them stiff. The vinegar slowly changes this

Bend the bone.

mineral so that the bone is no longer stiff. Try other kinds of bones as well to see if you can make them floppy. For a similar experiment, see experiment 2.

2
The bouncing egg

objective ☆ You can make an egg that will bounce. *Note:* This experiment will take a few days.

materials ☆ ❑ egg
❑ jar or glass
❑ 2 bottles of vinegar
❑ water from faucet
❑ saucepan
❑ stove

procedure ☆ 1. Have an adult make a hard-boiled egg for you. Allow the egg to cool.
2. Place the egg in a glass, and cover the egg with vinegar.

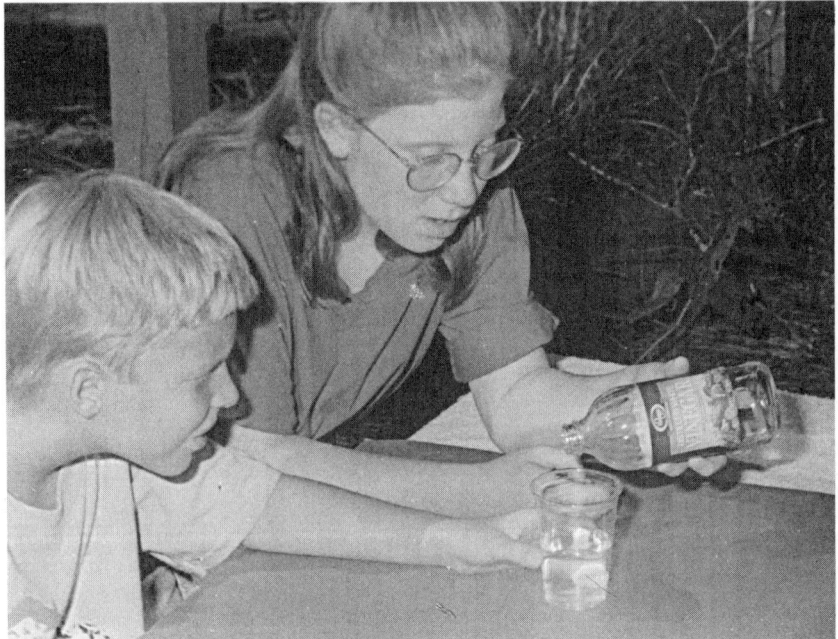

Pour vinegar into a glass.

3. Change the vinegar every 2 days.
4. After a few days, remove the egg from the vinegar.
5. Try dropping the egg. Does it bounce? Does the shell break?

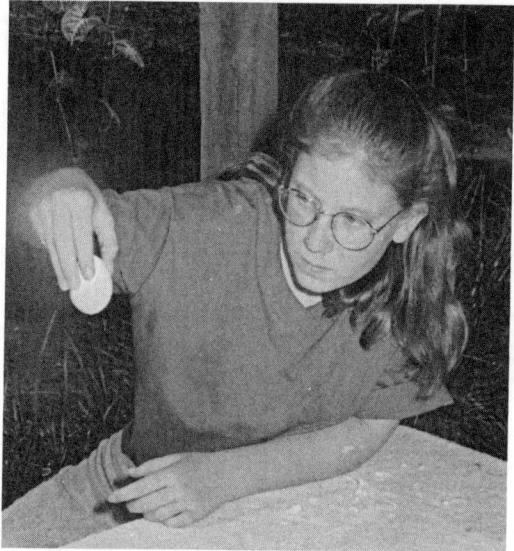

Drop the egg after soaking.

explanation ☆ Certain *minerals* in the egg shell make it hard. The vinegar removes these minerals, and the shell becomes soft, allowing the egg to bounce without breaking the shell.

3
Is it a liquid or solid?

objective ☆ When you mix cornstarch and water, you get a goo that seems to be both liquid and solid.

materials ☆
- ❏ measuring cup
- ❏ about ¾ cup cornstarch
- ❏ ½ cup water
- ❏ large bowl
- ❏ spoon
- ❏ newspaper

procedure ☆
1. Place newspapers on kitchen counter or table. Place the bowl on the newspaper.
2. Place ½ cup of water in the bowl.

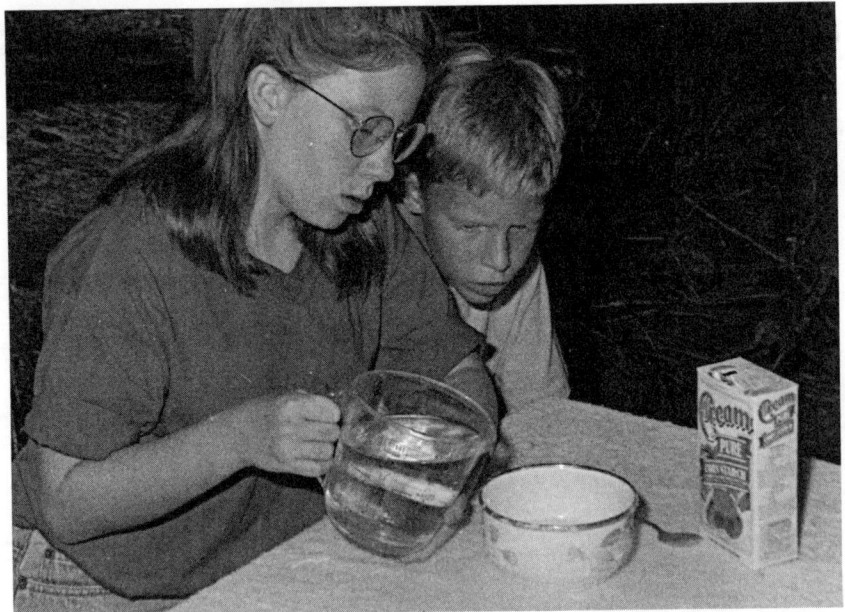

Add water to a bowl.

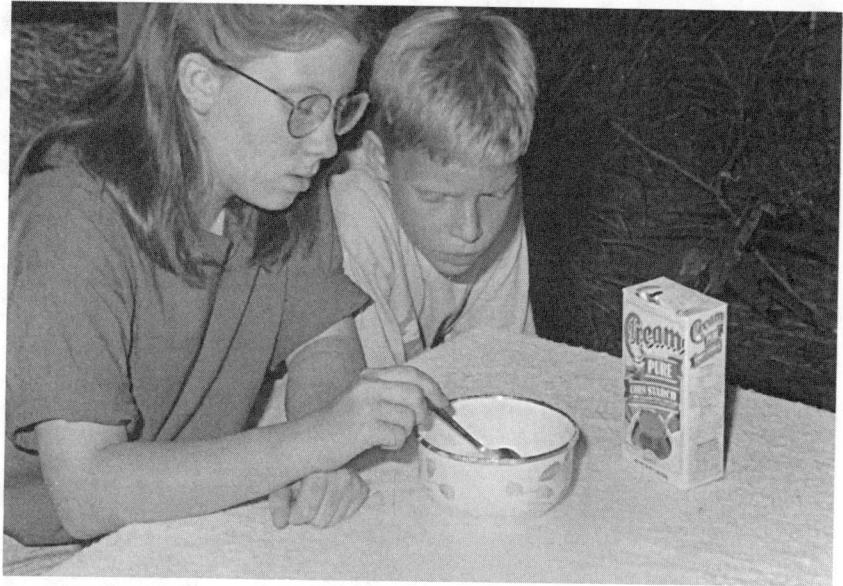

Stir the cornstarch.

3. Add about ½ cup of cornstarch to the water. Stir with a spoon.
4. Slowly add more cornstarch until the mix becomes very difficult to stir.
5. Grab the glob that you have made, and punch your finger into it. What happens?
6. Hold one end of the blob between your thumb and first finger and stretch it.
7. Roll the blob into a ball and place it on the counter. What happens to its shape?

explanation ☆ The mixture you made has properties of both liquids and solids. The *molecules* of cornstarch are very long and floppy. They can take on many different shapes as *gravity* pulls on them or as you mold them. They also absorb quite a bit of water and seem almost hard.

If a puddle or lake were made of cornstarch mix, do you think you could walk through it without sinking?

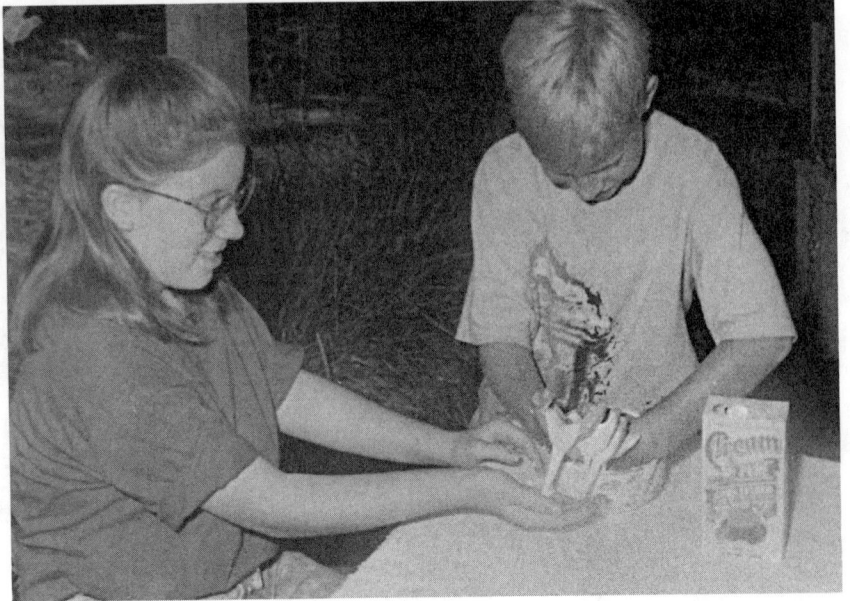

Hold the glob of goo.

Homemade Slime & Rubber Bones!

4
Homemade glue

objective ☆ You can make milk into glue. *Note:* This experiment may take about 30 minutes.

materials ☆
- ❏ measuring cup
- ❏ 2 cups of skim milk
- ❏ 6 tablespoons of vinegar
- ❏ ¼ cup water
- ❏ saucepan
- ❏ strainer
- ❏ small bowl
- ❏ small jar with lid
- ❏ 1 teaspoon baking soda
- ❏ teaspoon

procedure ☆
1. Pour 2 cups of skim milk into a saucepan.
2. Add 6 tablespoons of vinegar to the milk.
3. Have an adult heat the pan over medium heat on the stove.

Pan with "lumpy" milk.

4. Remove the pan from the heat when lumps begin to form.

Collect the lumps in a strainer.

Put the lump in a bowl.

5. Hold the strainer over the sink, and pour the "lumpy" milk through the strainer.

Making glue.

6. Use a teaspoon to press out any extra liquid from the lumps. You want these lumps to be as dry as possible.
7. Put the lumps in a small bowl.
8. Add ¼ cup of water and 1 teaspoon baking soda to the bowl.
9. Stir the mixture until everything dissolves.
10. Keep this mixture in a jar with a lid. Use it as glue.

explanation ☆ Heating the milk-vinegar mix caused the proteins in the milk to clump together or *precipitate*. These lumps are called *curd* and are very sticky.

Most cheeses are made by precipitation of the proteins present in milk. The flavor of the cheese comes from the chemicals made by the microorganisms that are added to the milk to form the curd.

5
The shriveled, slimy cup

objective ☆ A Styrofoam cup will shrivel or "melt" like the witch in the *Wizard of Oz*.

materials ☆
- ☐ Styrofoam cup
- ☐ fingernail-polish remover (containing acetone)
- ☐ cookie sheet, small pan, or small bowl

procedure ☆
1. Place the cup in the pan.
2. Fill the cup half-full with fingernail-polish remover.
3. Observe what happens to the cup.
4. Pick up the "melted" cup and roll it into a ball.

Pour the nail-polish remover into the cup.

Carefully pour water on top of the syrup.

A glass with three layers.

low density. The low-density liquid will float on top of the high-density liquid.

Which liquid had the lightest density? Which liquid had the heaviest density? For a similar experiment, see experiment 8.

8
Floating objects in liquids

objective ☆ You can make an art object that has different objects floating at different positions in a glass of liquid. *Note:* You should do experiment 7 before doing this one.

materials ☆
- ❏ tall glass or jar
- ❏ measuring cup
- ❏ syrup
- ❏ water from faucet
- ❏ cooking oil
- ❏ coin or metal washer
- ❏ grape
- ❏ few grains of rice
- ❏ cork

procedure ☆
1. Measure about 2 ounces (60 ml) of syrup and pour it into a tall glass.
2. Rinse the measuring cup many times with water until no more syrup remains.
3. Measure about 2 ounces (60 ml) of water and slowly pour this down the side of the glass. The water should stay on top of the syrup.
4. Measure about 2 ounces (60 ml) of cooking oil and slowly pour the oil down the side of the glass. It should float on top of the water. You should now have 3 layers in the glass. (See experiment 7.)
5. Slowly drop a coin down the side into the glass. What happens to the coin?
6. Drop a grape into the glass. What happens to the grape?

Homemade Slime & Rubber Bones!

7. Drop a few grains of rice into the glass. Where do the grains end up?
8. Drop the cork into the glass. Where does the cork end up?

Objects floating at different places.

explanation ☆ You formed three layers because the three liquids have different densities. A liquid with a lighter density will float on top of a liquid with a heavier density.

Objects will sink in liquids until they reach a liquid that has a density greater than itself. Another way to think of this is that lighter objects will sit on top of heavier objects. Which object has the highest density? Which object has the lowest density?

For another experiment with density, see experiment 9.

9
Floating an egg in water

objective ☆ You can float an egg in water.

materials ☆
- ❒ glass or wide-mouth jar
- ❒ uncooked egg
- ❒ salt
- ❒ water from faucet
- ❒ spoon

procedure ☆
1. Fill the glass half-full with water.
2. Carefully place the egg in the water. What happens to the egg?
3. Remove the egg from the glass.
4. Add about 10 spoonfuls of salt to the glass. Stir the salt until it all dissolves.
5. Carefully add the egg to the glass. What happens to the egg now?
6. If the egg still sinks, add a little more salt until it floats.

explanation ☆ Objects will sink in a liquid if the liquid has a lower density than the object. If the liquid is denser than the object, the object will float. You made the water have a higher density by adding the salt to the water.

It is easier for you to float in the ocean than in a pool or lake because the salt water is denser than fresh water. The Great Salt Lake in Utah has so much salt in it that it is almost impossible to sink at all.

After you have dissolved the salt in the water, add the egg.

Watch the egg float.

10
Layered colors

objective ☆ You can make 2 layers with different colors.

materials ☆ ❏ jar with lid
❏ measuring cup
❏ cooking oil
❏ water from faucet
❏ food coloring (blue or green works best)

procedure ☆ 1. Fill the jar half-full with water.
2. Add a few drops of food coloring.
3. Pour about 2 ounces (60 ml) of cooking oil into the jar.

Add water to the bottle.

Add food coloring to the water.

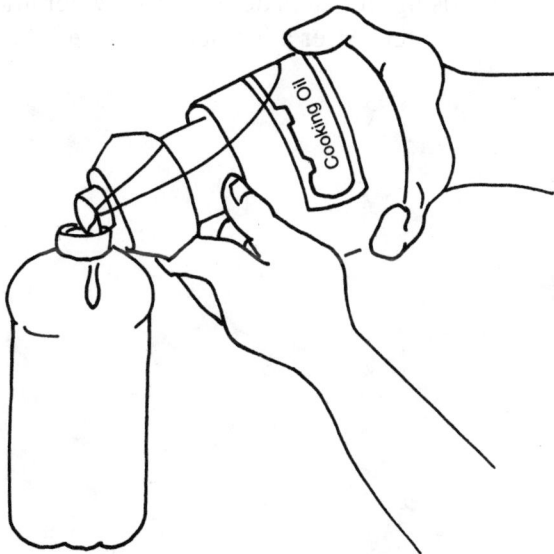

Add the oil to the bottle.

4. Put the lid on the jar.
5. Shake the jar a few seconds, then set the jar down.
6. Watch the jar for a few seconds. What do you see?

Shake the bottle.

explanation ☆ When you shook the jar, the oil was mixed with the water. But oil is lighter (less dense) than water and also does not mix well with water. After a few seconds, the oil rose to the top.

11
The wonders of egg whites

objective ☆ Egg whites can be used to help oil mix with water. *Note:* For a better understanding of this experiment, do experiment 10 first.

materials ☆
- ❐ jar or glass
- ❐ cooking oil
- ❐ egg
- ❐ bowl
- ❐ water from faucet
- ❐ spoon
- ❐ liquid dish detergent

procedure ☆
1. Ask an adult to separate the white from an egg for you. Put the egg whites in a bowl.
2. Fill the glass half-full with water.
3. Add 1 or 2 spoonfuls of cooking oil to the water. What happens to the oil?
4. Pour some of the egg white into the glass and stir.
5. What has happened to the oil now?
6. Wash and rinse the glass thoroughly.
7. Repeat steps 2 and 3.
8. Add a few drops of dish detergent and stir gently.
9. Observe what happens to the oil.

explanation ☆ If you have done experiments 7, 8, 9, or 10 you will recall that oils do not mix well with water. In fact, they do not react with water at all. They are said to be *hydrophobic*, which means the molecules of oil clump together to keep away as much water as possible.

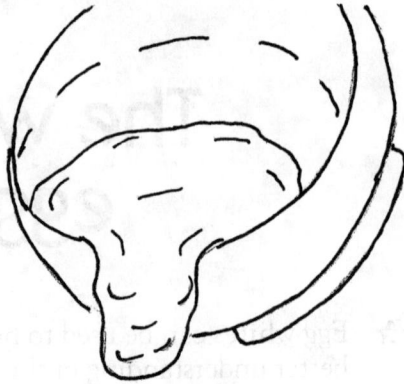

Add egg whites to the jar.

Stir the egg whites.

A chemical in the egg white acts by keeping the drops of oil from forming large clumps. It makes it easier for water to surround the small droplets of oil. Some of the chemicals in the dish detergent behave the same way as egg whites.

When we eat foods that have fats or oils in them, the fat in our blood behaves like the oil in the water. Sometimes these large drops of fat get caught in blood vessels and make it difficult for the blood to move through the vessels. When the vessels are narrowed or clogged, the heart has to pump harder to move the blood.

The chemical in egg white is also found in some other foods like eggplant. Can you think of any reason to include such foods in your diet?

12
How much water do things hold?

objective ☆ You will test how much water different materials will hold. *Note:* This experiment will take about 30 minutes.

materials ☆
- [ ] Styrofoam (not cardboard) egg carton OR plastic ice-cube tray
- [ ] cotton ball
- [ ] paper towel, 5 inches (12.5 cm) × 7 inches (17.5)
- [ ] square of disposable diaper, 1½ inches (4 cm) on a side
- [ ] teaspoon
- [ ] water from faucet
- [ ] paper & pencil

procedure ☆
1. Crumple the paper towel into a ball.
2. Place the cotton ball, paper towel, and diaper into separate compartments of egg carton or ice-cube tray.

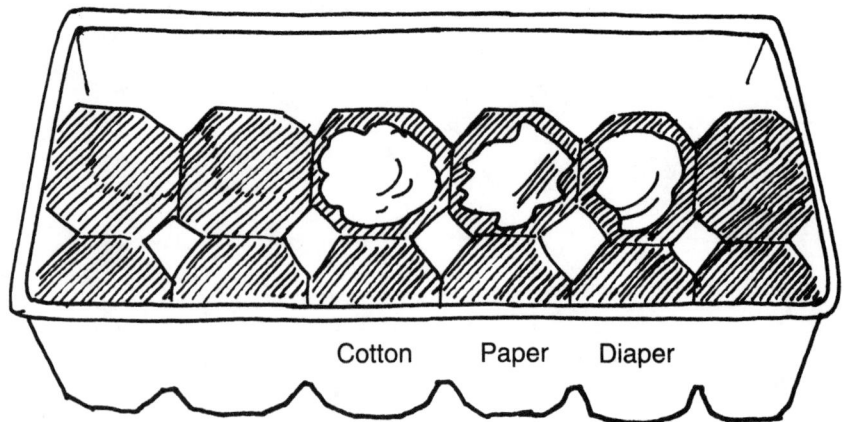

Cotton   Paper   Diaper

Place the materials in the egg carton.

3. Add 1 teaspoon of water to each material.
4. Lift each material to see if any water is in the compartment.
5. Repeat steps 3 and 4 until you see water in the compartment.
6. Write down how many teaspoons of water each material held.
7. Put your results on a graph like the one shown on page 34.

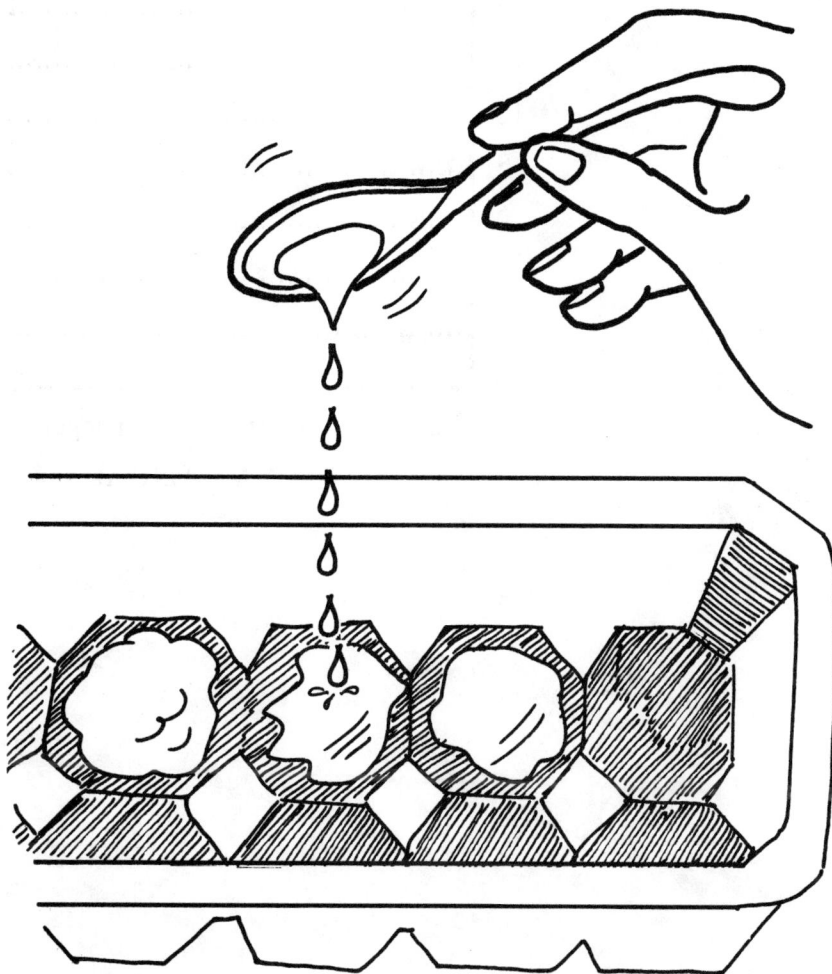

Add water to each material.

explanation ☆ Different materials will hold different amounts of water because of the shape of the fibers and the chemicals used to make the material. You can do this experiment with many different materials or different kinds of paper towels.

SPOONFULS

20
18
16
14
12
10
8
6
4
2
0

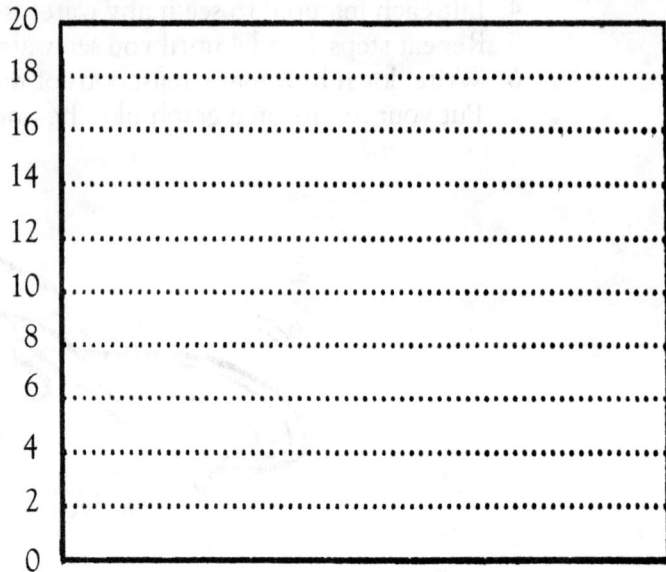

Towel   Cotton   Diaper   Other

MATERIAL

Part 3
Light & electricity

Light and electricity are forms of energy. Light travels through air at 186,000 miles (300,000 km) per second. When light passes from air into another material, such as water, it slows down. The result of this change is that the light is bent, and an object in water appears in a place different from its actual place.

All molecules have positive and negative *charges*. Normally, the number of positive and negative charges are equal. The molecule is neutral or has no charge.

When one type of charge moves, electricity results. Some objects can be made to gain or lose one kind of charge. When this happens, some objects will have a positive charge and others a negative charge. Objects with opposite charges will be *attracted* to each other.

important words
- ☆ attract
- ☆ charge
- ☆ circuit
- ☆ reflect
- ☆ repel
- ☆ static electricity

13
The bending pencil

objective ☆ A pencil in a glass of water appears bent or split.

materials ☆ ❑ glass
          ❑ pencil
          ❑ water from the faucet

procedure ☆ 1. Place the pencil in the empty glass. Does it appear straight?
          2. Remove the pencil.
          3. Fill the glass with water.

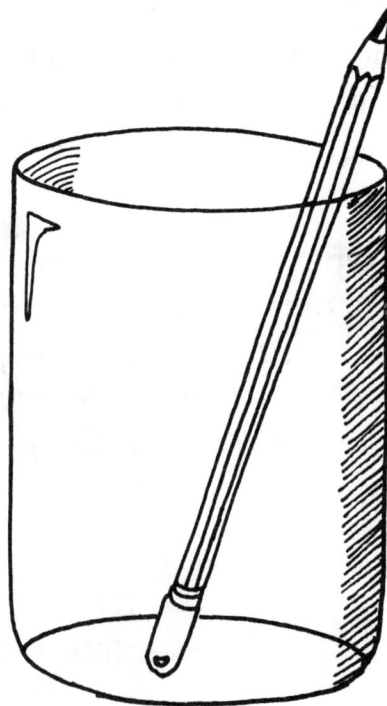

Place a pencil in an empty glass.

4. Place the pencil in the water.
5. Look at the glass from the side. Does the pencil appear straight?
6. Look at the glass from the top. How does the pencil appear?

Place a pencil in a glass of water.

explanation ☆ As light passes through different materials, it changes speed. The result is that the light is bent. When you placed the pencil in the water, the light traveled at different speeds through the air and the water, and the pencil appeared bent.

14
The repeating image

objective ☆ When you place mirrors correctly, you will see many images of the object.

materials ☆ ❏ 2 identical-sized mirrors, at least 2 inches (5 cm) square
❏ coin, eraser, or other object
❏ 2 books (optional)

procedure ☆ 1. Place the 2 mirrors upright about 4 inches (10 cm) apart. You may find it easier to rest them against a book.
2. Place the object between the mirrors.
3. Look into one of the mirrors. How many images do you see?
4. Try moving the mirrors farther apart to see if you still see the same number of images.

Place two mirrors upright.

explanation ☆ Light from each mirror is *reflected* to make an image. Each reflected image makes another image, and these reflected images make still more images.

Many images in a mirror.

15
Sticking balloons to the wall

objective ☆ You can stick a balloon to the wall without using tape.

materials ☆ ☐ blown-up balloon

procedure ☆ 1. Rub the balloon across your shirt or hair 10 to 20 times.

Rub the balloon 10 to 20 times.

2. Place the rubbed side of the balloon to the wall.
3. Let go of the balloon. Does it stick to the wall?

explanation ☆ Rubbing the balloon created *static electricity*. The charge on the balloon was attracted to the opposite charge on the wall. The balloon may remain on the wall for 5 or 10 minutes. For other experiments with static electricity, see experiments 16 and 17.

16
Dancing pepper

objective ☆ Pepper on a sheet of paper will suddenly jump up to a balloon.

materials ☆
- ☐ paper towel
- ☐ pepper
- ☐ inflated balloon

procedure ☆
1. Sprinkle some pepper on a paper towel.
2. Rub the balloon across your shirt or hair 10 to 20 times.
3. Hold the balloon a short distance above the pepper. Do not touch the balloon to the pepper.
4. Observe what happens to the pepper.

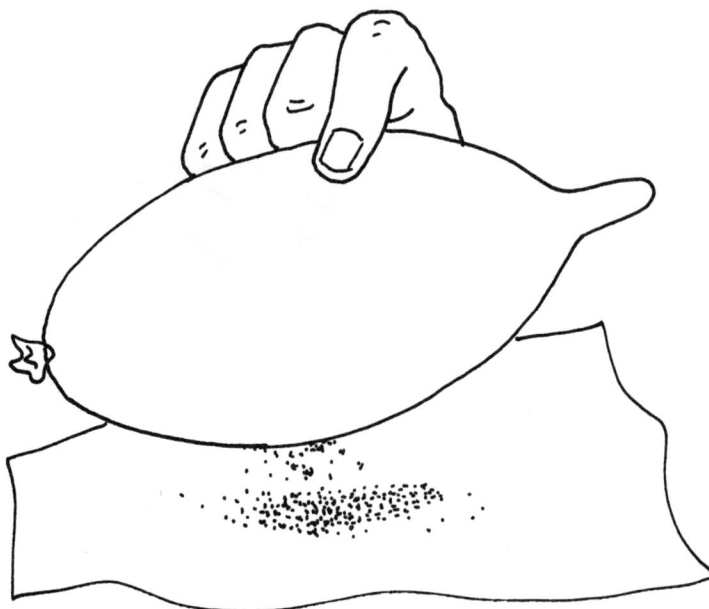

Hold the balloon over the pepper.

explanation ☆ When you rubbed the balloon, you created *static electricity*. Static electricity results from creating a charge on something. The charge on the balloon attracted the oppositely charged pepper, and the pepper moved to the balloon.

Try other spices to see if they will jump. Can you think of any uses of static electricity?

17
Moving a can
with a balloon

objective ☆ You can move a soft drink can with a balloon.

materials ☆ ❑ blown-up balloon
❑ empty soft drink can

procedure ☆ 1. Place the can on the top of the counter or table.
2. Rub the balloon 10 to 20 times across your shirt or hair.

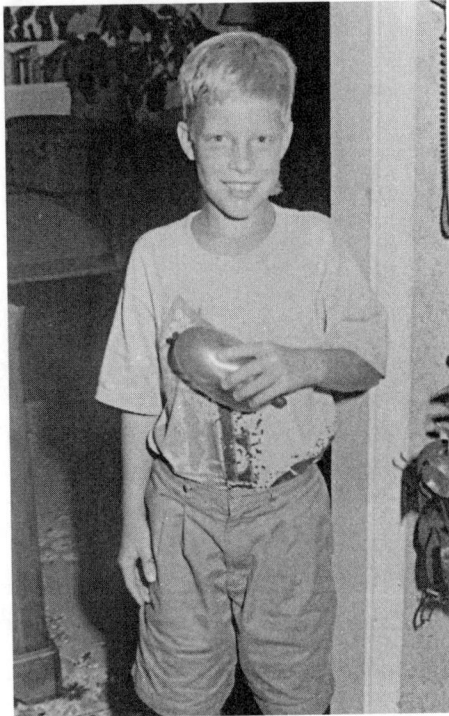

Rub the balloon 10 to 20 times.

3. Hold the balloon a short distance above the can. Be sure not to touch the balloon to the can.
4. Slowly begin to move the balloon and see what happens to the can.

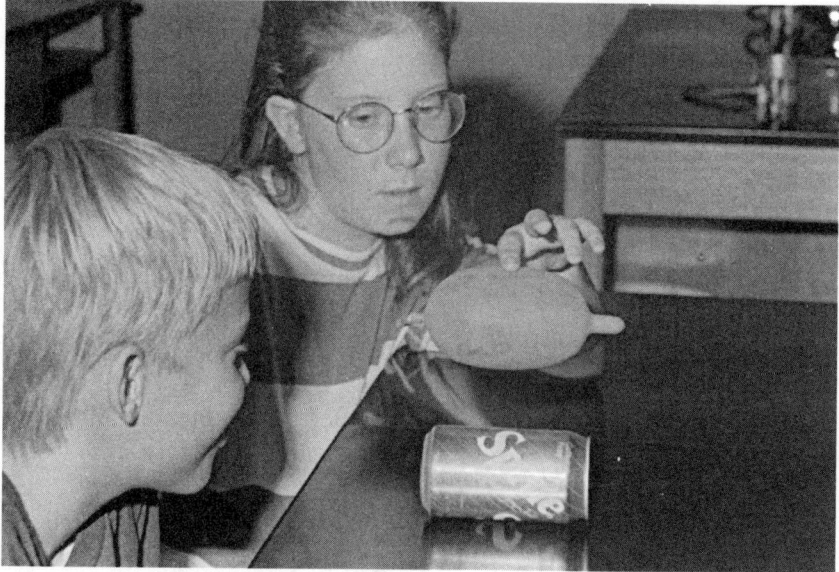

Hold the balloon near the can.

explanation ☆ Rubbing the balloon created a *charge*, or a quantity of electricity, on the balloon. If the charge on the balloon is the same as the charge on the can, the can is *repelled* or moved away from the balloon. If the charge on the balloon is different from the charge on the can, the can is *attracted* to the balloon, and moves toward it.

18
The shocking lemon

objective ☆ You can produce a small shock from a lemon.

materials ☆
- ☐ lemon
- ☐ paper clip
- ☐ penny or other copper coin

procedure ☆
1. Have an adult make two small slits in a lemon with a knife. One slit must be about ¼ inch (5 mm) from the other slit.
2. Place a paper clip in one slit and a penny in the other slit of the lemon.
3. Touch your tongue to the penny and the paper clip. Do you feel a small tingling?

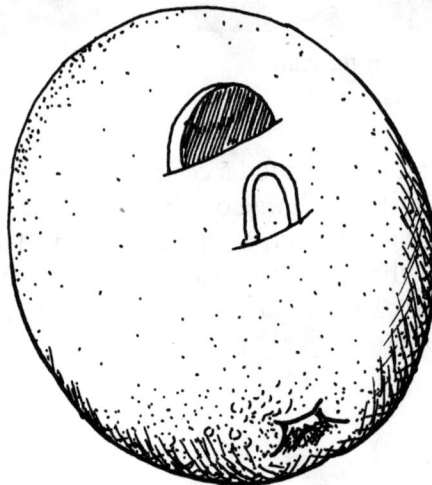

A lemon with a paper clip and penny.

Touch the tongue to the metals.

explanation ☆ Electricity can be made by placing two different metals in acid. The paper clip is made of steel, and the penny is made of copper. Your tongue served as a bridge to allow electricity to flow in a complete *circuit* or cycle.

Car batteries work on this same principle; they are made by placing alternating plates of different metals in an acid.

Part 4
Biology

Biology is the study of living things. Living things require energy and can respond to different types of signals. In this section, you will see how plants move water, how the human body responds to different signals, and how heat changes the behavior of things inside of cells.

important
words

- ☆ average
- ☆ bacteria
- ☆ enzyme
- ☆ reaction time
- ☆ sensor

19
The case of
disappearing water

objective ☆   When a stem of a plant is placed in a glass of water, some of the water disappears. *Note:* This experiment will go on for at least 24 hours.

materials ☆
- ❑ 3 glasses or jars
- ❑ 3 cups water (from faucet)
- ❑ 3 ounces cooking oil (90 ml)
- ❑ measuring cup
- ❑ marking pen
- ❑ plant stem with at least 6 leaves (a small branch from a young tree also works)
- ❑ plant stem with no leaves

procedure ☆
1. Pour 1 cup (230 ml) of water into each glass.
2. Gently pour 1 ounce (30 ml) of cooking oil on top of the water in each glass.
3. Place the stem with leaves in one glass and the stem without leaves in another glass. Be sure the stems are near the bottom of the glass.
4. Mark the level of water in each glass.
5. Place all glasses on the counter until the next day.
6. Determine the water level in each glass on the next day. Are they all the same?
7. Examine the glasses for 1 or 2 more days.

explanation ☆   Water travels up the stem of a plant to the leaves. The water in the leaf evaporates into the air. This experiment shows that leaves help pull water up through the stem. You probably observed that only the plant with leaves showed a loss of water. The oil on top of

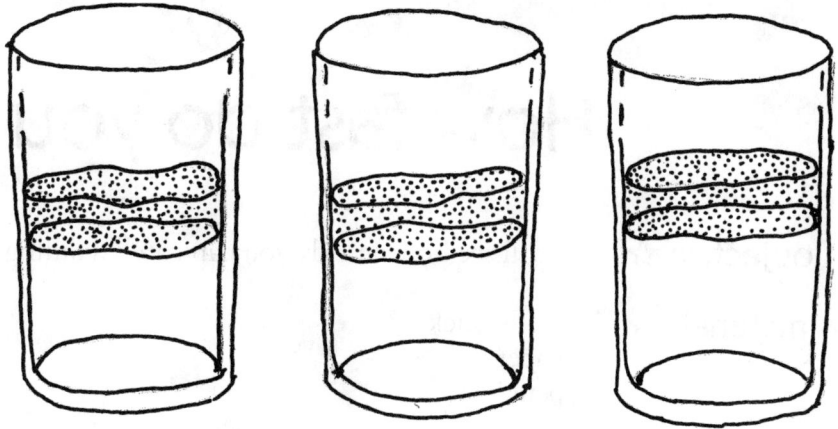

Fill three glasses with water and then oil.

Place the stems in two of the glasses.

the water prevented the water from evaporating into the air by itself.

This experiment was first done over 300 years ago by Stephen Hales. He was the first person to show that leaves are necessary for water to move from the roots up the stem to the leaves.

20
How fast do you react?

objective ☆ You will see how quickly you can catch a falling stick.

materials ☆
- ❒ meter stick
- ❒ paper
- ❒ pencil

procedure ☆
1. Hold the meter stick near one end as shown. The top of your hand should be about at the 20-centimeter mark.
2. Open your hand and let the stick drop.

Grasp the meter stick near the bottom.

3. As quickly as possible, close your hand to catch the stick.
4. Note the number in centimeters where your hand caught the stick.

Catch the falling stick.

5. Subtract the starting distance from the ending distance.
6. Multiply this number by 4.
7. Add 90 to the number you got in step 6. Now divide this number by 1000.
8. Write down this number from step 7. This is your reaction time in seconds.
9. Repeat steps 1 to 8 two more times.
10. Add all three reaction times.
11. Divide the number in step 10 by 3. This is your *average* reaction time.

Example:

The stick fell from 20 cm to 45 cm before it was caught.

$$45-20 \quad = \quad 25$$
$$25 \times 4 \quad = \quad 100$$
$$100+90 \quad = \quad 190$$
$$190 \div 1000 \quad = \quad 0.190 \text{ seconds}$$

explanation ☆ When scientists do experiments, they usually try to do them more than once to see if they get about the same results each time. Results are never exactly the same, so scientists determine the *average* result. You calculate averages in school when you add up all your tests and divide by the number of tests.

Were all three of your reaction times close to each other, or were they very different? If they were different, can you think of a reason for this difference?

Have your friends or family determine their reaction times. Which one had the fastest reaction time? Which one had the slowest reaction time?

21
Determining where you were touched

objective ☆ You will try to determine where a person has touched you. *Note:* This experiment requires 2 people.

materials ☆
- ❑ 2 different-colored, washable marking pens
- ❑ ruler
- ❑ pencil & paper

procedure ☆ 1. Close your eyes. Your partner should touch your arm with one of the marking pens.

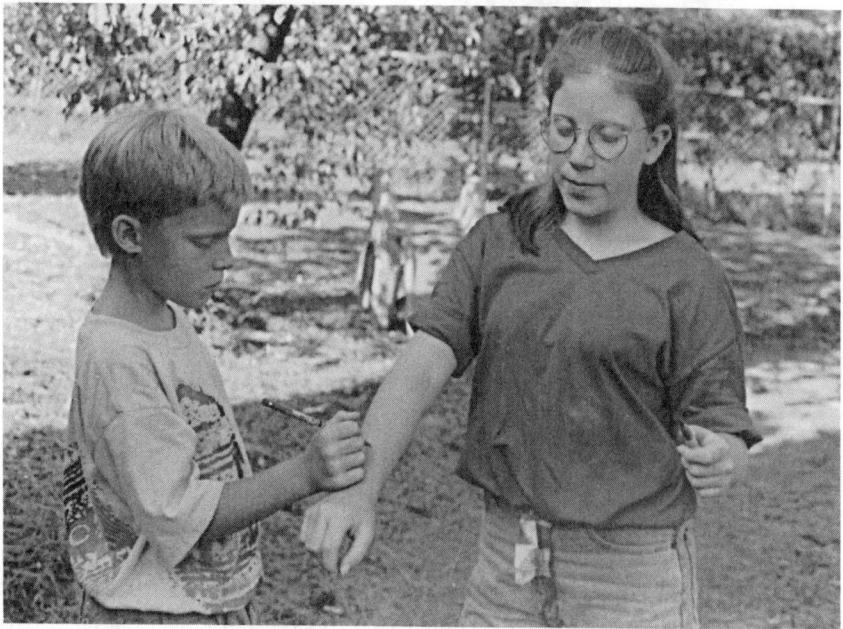

Make the first mark.

2. Keeping your eyes closed and using the other marker, try to make a mark as close as possible to the first touch. Be sure to keep your eyes closed when doing this step.

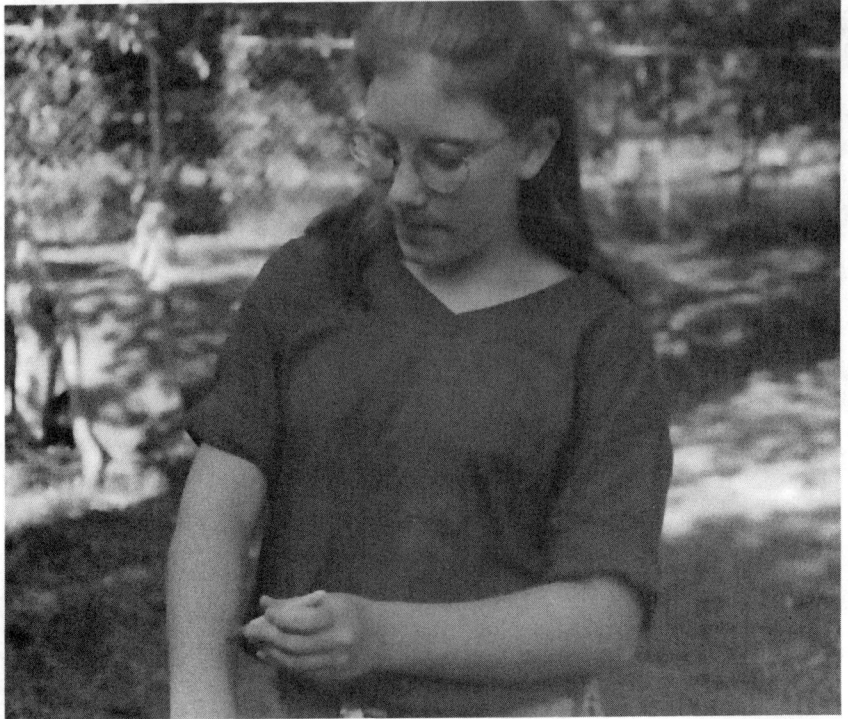

Try to touch near the first mark.

3. Measure in millimeters the distance between the colored dots. Record the distance.
4. Repeat steps 1 to 3 on other parts of the body: the chest, the abdomen or stomach, the forehead, the back of the neck, the arm, the bottom of the feet.
5. On which part of the body can you best locate touch?
6. Have your partner now try to touch as close as where you have touched.

explanation ☆ Different parts of the body have different numbers of touch *sensors*. Your dots will be closer together on those parts of the body that have many touch sensors. Where are many sensors located? Where are few sensors found?

22
Changing body temperatures

objective ☆ When you eat or drink something hot or cold, the temperature of your fingers changes. *Note:* Each part of this experiment will take about 30 minutes.

materials ☆
❒ thermometer (the kind you put in your mouth is fine)
❒ 16 ounces (500 ml) warm water or tea
❒ 16 ounces (500 ml) ice water
❒ paper & pencil

procedure ☆
1. Hold the bulb of the thermometer between your thumb and index finger.
2. Record the temperature.
3. As quickly as you can, drink the hot water. The water or tea should be just slightly cooler than freshly made coffee or tea. You want to try to drink all the liquid within 5 to 10 minutes.

Drink some ice water.

4. When you have drunk about half of the liquid, grasp the thermometer again and measure the temperature. Write it down.

Measure the temperature of your fingers.

5. Continue drinking the liquid until it is all gone.
6. Measure and record the temperature when all the liquid is gone.
7. Wait 5 minutes, then measure and record the temperature again. How has the temperature of your fingers changed during this experiment?
8. Wait about 30 minutes.
9. Now repeat steps 2 to 7, but this time, drink the ice water.

explanation ☆ You were probably surprised that the temperature of your finger is less than your "normal" body temperature. Much heat is lost through the fingers, and they are usually a few degrees cooler than the inside of your body.

When you drink something hot or cold, the liquid quickly enters the blood. When this happens, the temperature of the blood changes slightly. This blood with a different temperature is quickly pumped throughout your body.

When you are outside in cold weather, do you think it would be better to drink warm or cold liquids? Why?

23
Bubbles on meat

objective ☆ When hydrogen peroxide is put on 2 pieces of meat, bubbles form on only one of the pieces.

materials ☆
- ❏ 2 small pieces of meat
- ❏ pan
- ❏ stove
- ❏ hydrogen peroxide (available in grocery and drug stores)
- ❏ teaspoon
- ❏ plate

procedure ☆

1. Have an adult cook thoroughly one of the pieces of meat.
2. Place both pieces of meat on a plate.
3. Put 1 teaspoon of hydrogen peroxide on each piece of meat.
4. Look for the presence of bubbles on the meat.

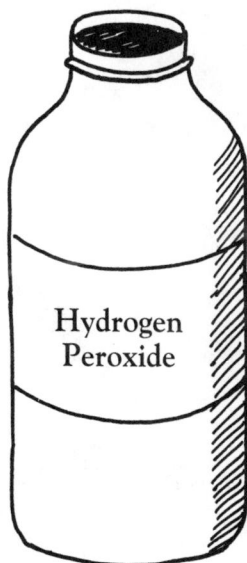

Place some hydrogen peroxide on some meat.

explanation ☆ Cells contain protein molecules called *enzymes*. These enzymes cause chemical reactions inside of cells. A particular enzyme breaks down hydrogen peroxide into water and oxygen. The bubbles that you saw were bubbles of oxygen.

When things are heated, most enzymes are destroyed and can no longer work. The cooked meat did not produce any bubbles.

Heat can be used to kill *bacteria* in foods. The heat destroys the enzymes of the bacteria so the bacteria can no longer grow. Why might it be important to destroy bacteria in foods?

24
Making fingerprints

objective ☆ You can use pencil lead to detect fingerprints.

materials ☆
- ☐ sandpaper
- ☐ pencil
- ☐ small paintbrush
- ☐ paper
- ☐ glass or other object

procedure ☆
1. Rub the pencil lead across the sandpaper many times.
2. Carefully transfer the powder to a sheet of paper.
3. Touch a glass or other object.

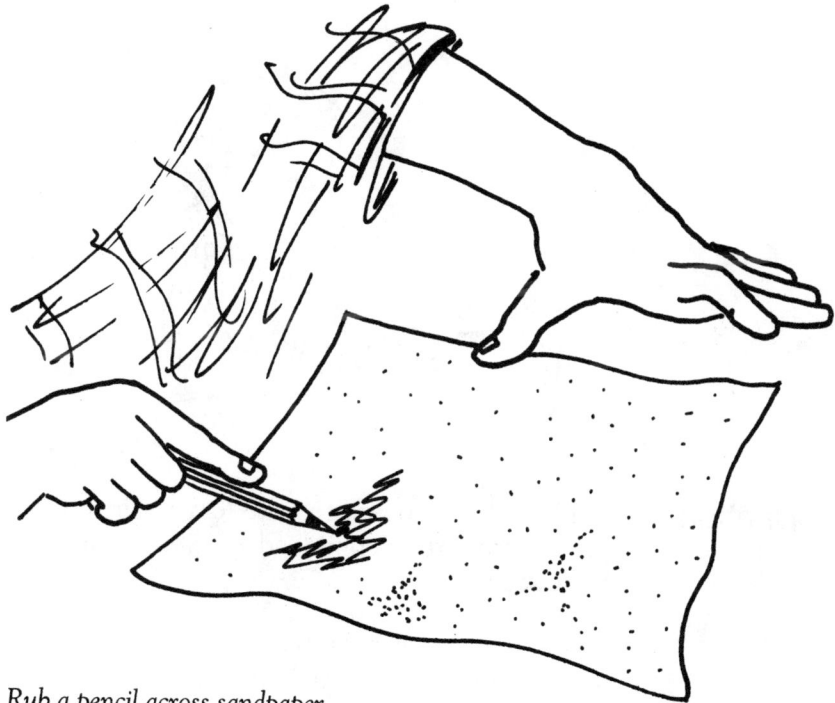

Rub a pencil across sandpaper.

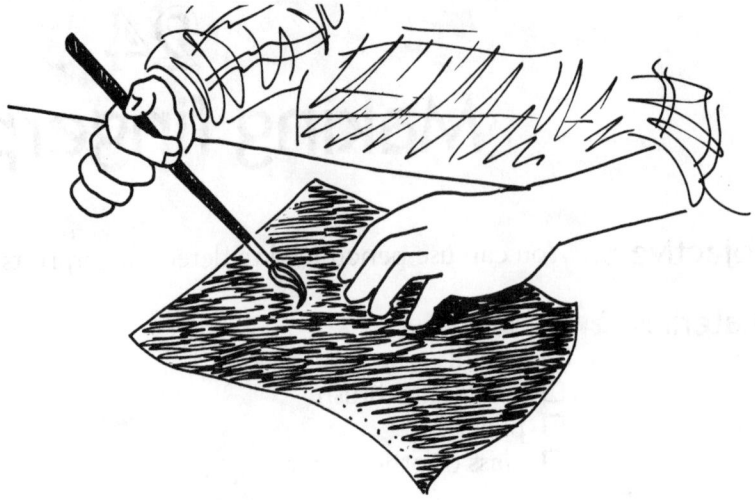

Put some lead on a paintbrush.

4. With the paintbrush, carefully, "paint" some of the powder over the glass. Do not use too much pencil lead.
5. Look at the glass for your fingerprint.

"Paint" some pencil lead on a glass.

explanation ☆ Oil from your fingers helps to leave a fingerprint on an object. The powder from the pencil lead allowed the image of your fingerprint to be seen.

You might also want to try something like talcum powder to see if it will help you see fingerprints.

Part 5
Motion, weight, & balance

Motion results when a *force*, (a push or pull) is applied to an object. This force can come from many sources; air, gravity, machines, etc.

In order for objects to be balanced on another object, the mass must be distributed evenly around a point. Many experiments in this section involve the distribution of mass.

A very important rule of motion is the *Law of Inertia*. It says that an object in motion will tend to stay in motion, and an object at rest will tend to stay at rest, unless a force is applied to the object. As you do the experiments in this section, try to figure out what types of forces are working and whether they are pushing or pulling.

important words

- ☆ center of gravity
- ☆ corrugated paper
- ☆ displace
- ☆ force
- ☆ inertia
- ☆ rigid

25
Rolling up a hill

objective ☆ An object placed on the bottom of a ramp magically rolls up the ramp.

materials ☆
- ☐ 2 same-sized funnels, OR 2 cone-shaped paper cups
- ☐ 2 strips of wood or cardboard, about 3 feet (1 meter) long
- ☐ 5 books
- ☐ tape

procedure ☆
1. Tape the funnels together.
2. Place one end of each wood or cardboard strip on top of one book. The ends of the strips should be very close together.

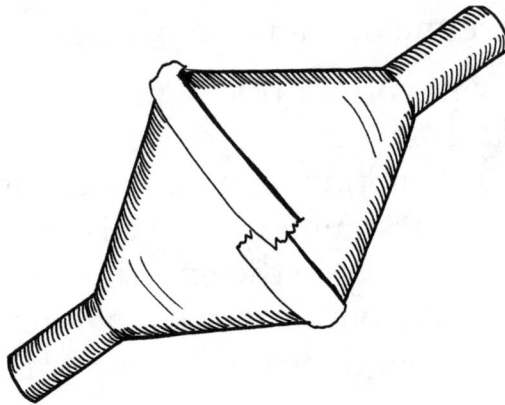

Tape the funnels together.

3. Place the other ends of the strips on top of two books. These ends should be about 3 to 4 inches (7–10 cm) apart.
4. Place a book on top of each of the strips.
5. Place the taped funnels between the lower end of the strips.
6. Observe what happens to the funnels.

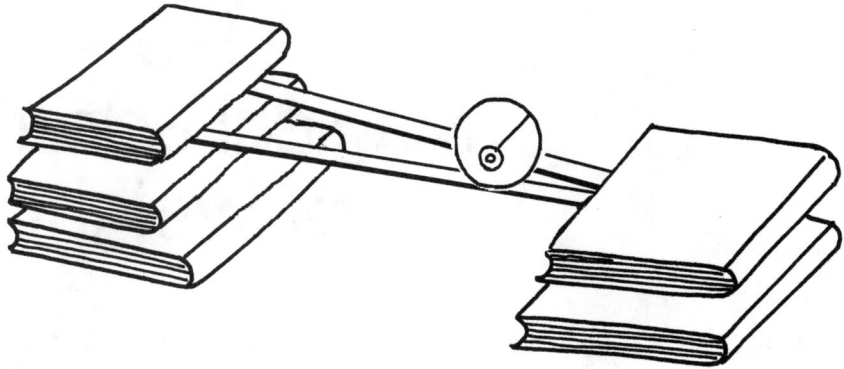

Place the funnels on the strips.

explanation ☆ The funnels don't actually roll uphill; they just seem to. Try looking at the funnels from the side as they move. The thickest part of the funnel is higher than the high end of the strips. This part of the funnel is its *center of gravity*. An object with a high center of gravity will move to a place or position with a lower center of gravity. By doing this, the object becomes more stable.

To help you think about the center of gravity, think about two glasses or vases—one with a narrow base and wide top, and the other with a large base and narrow top. The first one is less stable and is easily knocked over because more weight is at the top.

You might have to try placing the funnels in different places in order to get them to roll.

26
Magical addition of weight

objective ☆ Placing your finger in a cup of water makes the cup heavier.

materials ☆
- ❑ 2 Styrofoam cups
- ❑ ruler, at least 6 inches (15 cm) long
- ❑ pencil
- ❑ water from faucet

procedure ☆
1. Fill each cup half-full with water.
2. Place the ruler on the pencil so the pencil is under the middle of the ruler.
3. Place a cup on each end of the ruler. Move the cups until they are balanced.
4. Place your finger into one of the cups. What happens to the ruler? Is it still balanced?

explanation ☆ When you place anything in water, some of the water is moved or *displaced* to make room for the object. This displacement has the effect of making the water heavier. Even though your finger was just dipped in the water, the cup had added weight.

Balance the cups on a ruler.

Place your finger in one cup.

27
A strangely falling coin

objective ☆ Show a friend that you can make a coin fall into a jar without touching the coin.

materials ☆
- ☐ jar
- ☐ coin
- ☐ index card
- ☐ pencil (optional)

procedure ☆
1. Place the index card over the top of the jar.
2. Place the coin in the middle of the card.

Place the coin on the index card.

3. Flick your finger quickly against the edge of the card. Your finger must push the card horizontally, not upward or downward. Another option is to use the pencil to quickly hit the edge of the card.
4. Observe what happens to the coin.

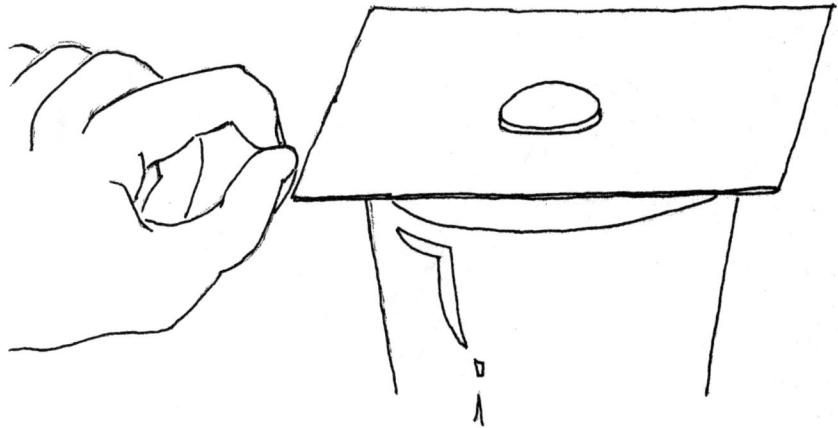

Flick the card with your finger.

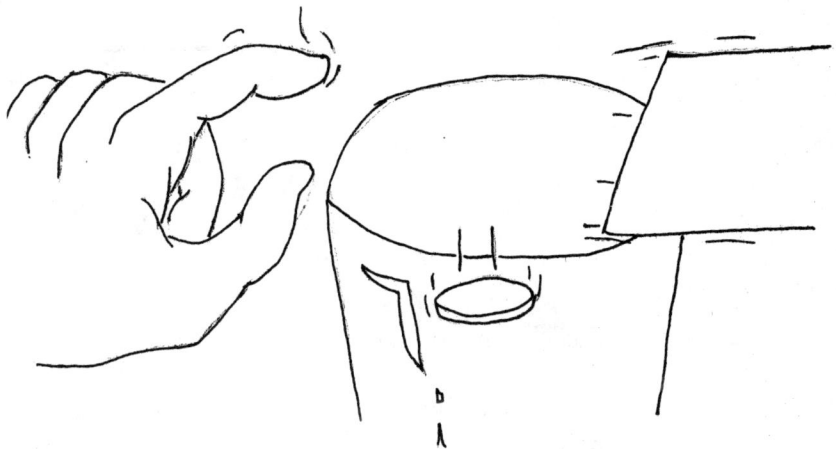

Watch the coin fall.

explanation ☆ This experiment shows that an object at rest (the coin) tends to stay at rest. This property is called *inertia*. When you hit the card, it started to move, but the coin did not. The coin fell into the jar.

This experiment will take some practice to be able to hit the card from the correct direction. When the card moves, it must stay flat.

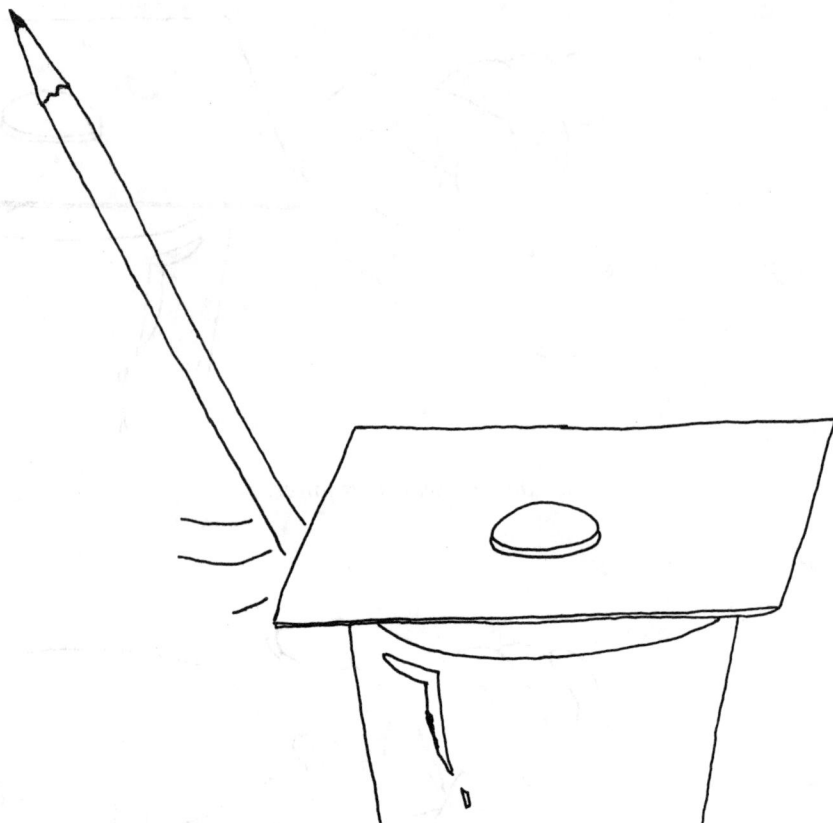

Flick the card with a pencil.

The Law of Inertia was discovered by Isaac Newton. The other part of the law says that objects in motion tend to stay in motion. If you are riding in a car and the car suddenly stops, you are often thrown forward. You were in motion and kept moving when the car stopped.

For other experiments with inertia, see experiments 28 and 29.

28
Putting a nail into a jar

objective ☆ A nail, balanced on a ring, suddenly falls into a jar.

materials ☆ ❏ narrow-mouth jar, such as a soft-drink bottle
❏ roll of tape OR embroidery hoop
❏ nail, about 3 inches (7–8 cm) long

procedure ☆ 1. Place the roll of tape on top of the bottle.
2. Carefully balance the nail on top of the tape. The nail must be over the opening of the jar.
3. Place your thumb and index finger inside the roll of tape.

Balance the nail on the roll.

4. Flick your finger against the inside of the tape roll. If you hit the tape at the right spot, the nail will fall into the jar. This experiment will probably require many tries to get the proper motion for hitting the tape.

Flick the inside of the roll.

explanation ☆ This experiment is another example of *inertia* (see experiment 27), but possibly a little more exciting. When you hit the tape, there was nothing to support the nonmoving nail, and it fell into the jar.

Do not be discouraged if the nail does not fall the first few times. This experiment requires practice. It will not work if you hit the tape from the outside.

29
Pushing a straw
through a potato

objective ☆ With practice, you can push a straw through a potato.

materials ☆ ❑ potato
❑ straw

procedure ☆ 1. Place your thumb over the end of the straw.
2. Hold the potato in your other hand.

*Hold your thumb over
the straw.*

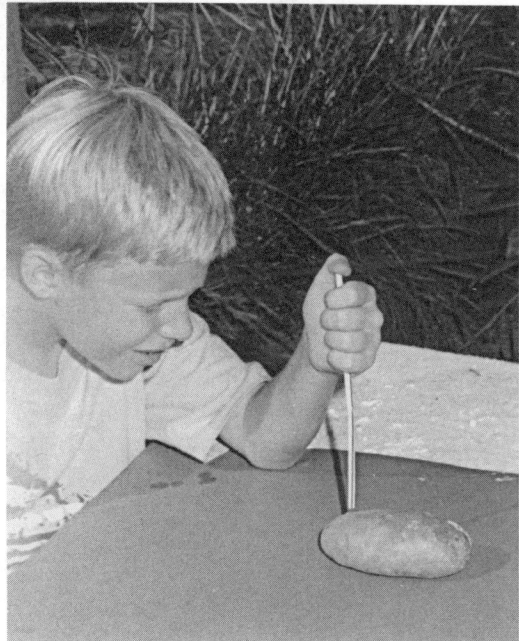

3. Quickly push the straw into the potato.
4. Observe what happens to the straw. Do you think the same thing will happen if you do not put your thumb on the end of the straw?

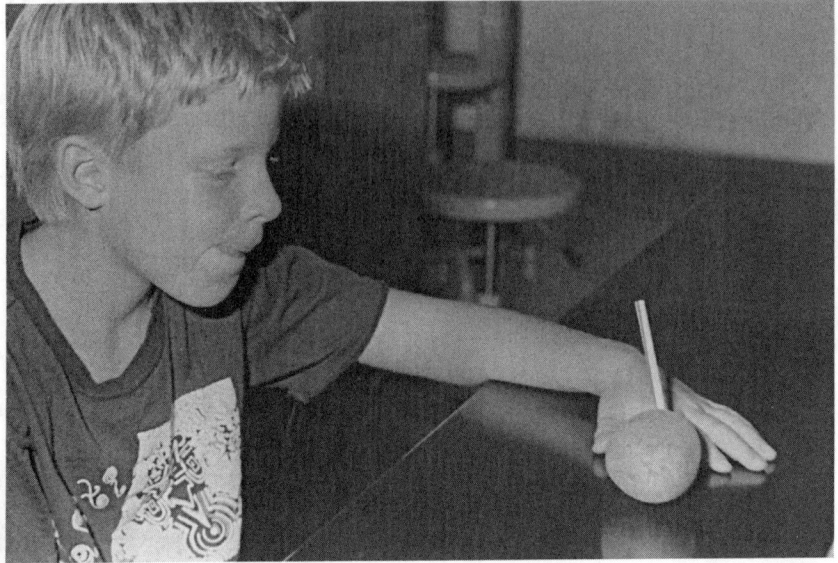

Push the straw into the potato.

explanation ☆ The straw is flexible, but when you cover one end, air is trapped in the straw. The air makes the straw *rigid*, or stiff, and allows it to be pushed into the potato.

You might have to practice this experiment many times in order to determine the correct position for the straw. Try other foods, such as an orange or a squash, to see if they work.

30
Balancing nails

objective ☆ Challenge a friend to balance 10 or 12 nails on one other nail. He or she probably will be unable to do it, but you will!

materials ☆
- ❏ piece of wood, at least 1½ inches (4 cm) thick
- ❏ 12 or 13 nails, at least 4 inches (10 cm) long
- ❏ hammer

procedure ☆ 1. Have an adult pound a nail into the wood. The nail must be straight and should not come through the other side of the wood.

Pound the nail into the wood.

Balance the nail.

2. Try to balance 1 nail on the nail in the block.
3. Now try to balance the second nail. It will probably fall off.
4. Lay the first nail on the table.
5. Place the other nails on top of it as shown.
6. Pick up the nails and carefully place them on the nail in the wood.
7. All the nails should now be balanced on the first nail.

explanation ☆ To balance objects, you must distribute the mass evenly around a point. The structure you made distributes the mass evenly on each side of the nail in the wood.

Arrange the nails.

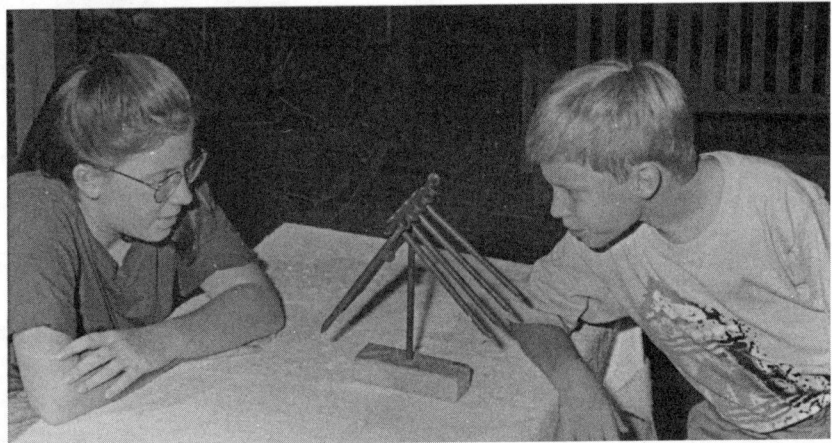

Balance all of the nails.

31
The paper bridge

objective ☆ Bet a friend that with 1 sheet of paper you can make a bridge that will hold up a book.

materials ☆
- ❏ sheet of paper
- ❏ 2 same-sized books or pieces of wood
- ❏ another book

procedure ☆
1. Arrange the boards so that they are about 4 inches (10 cm) apart.
2. Place the sheet of paper across the space.
3. Place the book on the paper. What happens to the book?
4. Take the piece of paper and fold it back and forth to make a fan. The paper should have many creases in it.

Fold the paper.

5. Place the folded paper across the boards.
6. Place a book on the folded paper. What happens to the book this time?

Place the folded paper on the books.

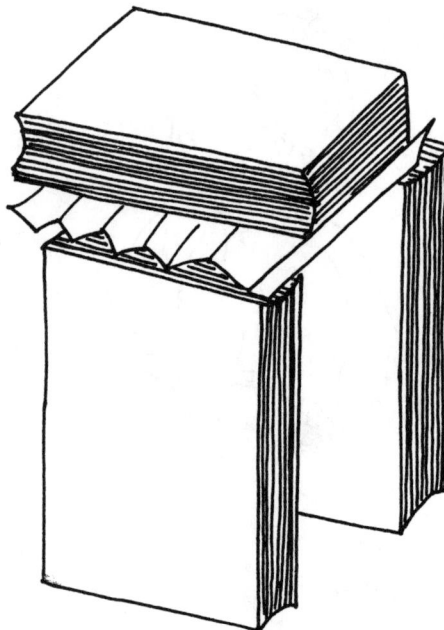

Place a book on the folded paper.

explanation ☆ When you folded the paper, you made something called *corrugated* paper. If you look at the folded paper, you will see many triangles. The points of the triangle allow the mass to be distributed over many different areas. Such a shape will support heavier objects than will a flat structure.

Why do you think many cardboard boxes are made with corrugated paper?

32
The powerful cylinder

objective ☆ You can support a book on one sheet of paper.

materials ☆ ❑ sheet of paper
❑ tape
❑ 1 or more books

procedure ☆ 1. Roll the paper into a tube, or cylinder.
2. Tape the edges together.
3. Stand the tube on end.

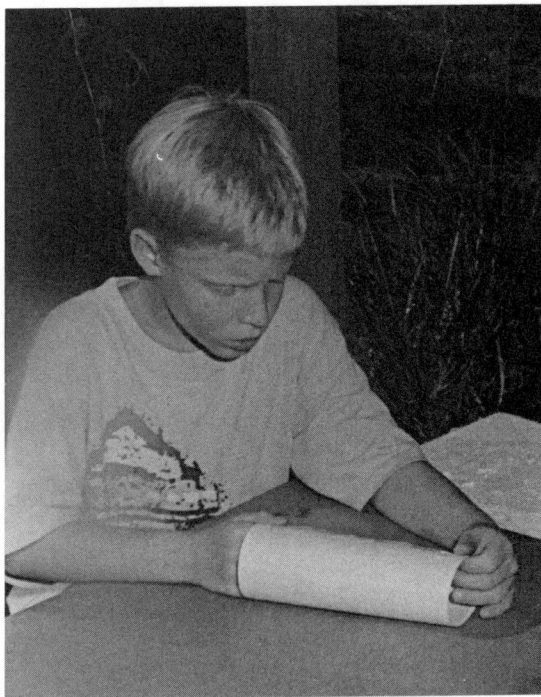

Make a cylinder.

4. Place a book on top of the tube. Does the tube collapse?
5. Add more books until the tube collapses.

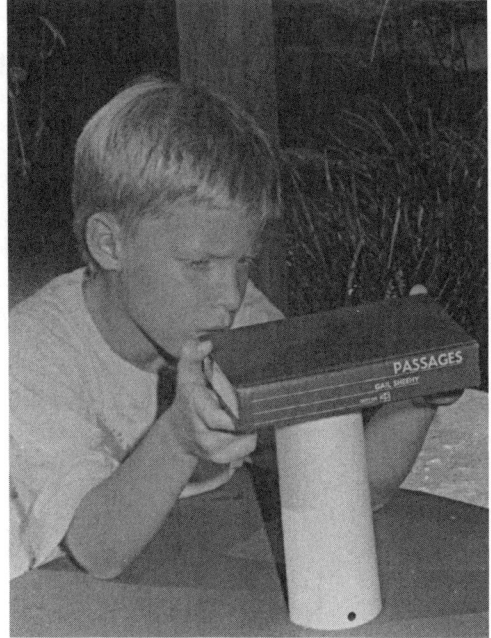

Place a book on the cylinder.

explanation ☆ The mass of an object is distributed evenly around the edges of a circle and also downward. Cylinders or columns are very strong and can support much mass.

Look at the shape of a leg bone from an animal. Notice that it is almost round. Why do you think the leg bone of a cow has a larger diameter than the leg bone of a human?

33
How strong
are eggshells?

objective ☆ Eggshells break very easily, but you will see that they are actually quite strong.

materials ☆
- ❏ 4 halves of eggshells (from 2 eggs)
- ❏ scissors
- ❏ 1 or more books

procedure ☆
1. Have an adult crack 2 or more eggs. Try to crack each egg into 2 equal pieces. (Save the egg whites to do experiment 11.)
2. With the scissors, trim the edge of each half until it is flat and even.

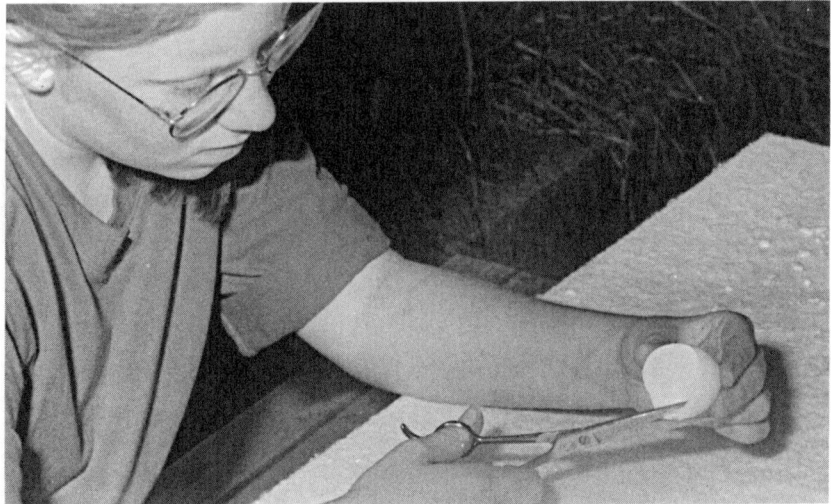

Cut an eggshell in half.

3. When you have 4 equal-sized halves, place them to form the corners of a square.
4. Place a book on top of the shells. Do the shells crack?
5. If the shells do not crack, keep adding books until they do.

Balance a book on the shells.

explanation ☆ Shapes that resemble a half sphere are very strong because much of the weight is not distributed straight down, but rather out to the sides. This principle is used to make domes and igloos.

Part 6
Crystals, cleaning, & water

Crystals are a pure form of a compound. Different compounds form different-shaped crystals. Many crystals can be dissolved in water. The amount of crystal dissolved depends on the chemical. When water evaporates, crystals will reform. The amount of chemical dissolved in water depends on temperature. More of a chemical will usually dissolve in hot water than in cold water.

Certain chemicals react to form acids. Some acids can react with other chemicals and cause them to change into new compounds. This change can often be seen by a change in appearance, such as loss of color. Heat can also cause some chemicals to change.

important words
☆ crystal
☆ evaporate
☆ solubility

34
Candy on a string

objective ☆ You can make your own rock candy. *Note:* This experiment will take about a week to complete.

materials ☆
- ❏ 1 cup water (from faucet)
- ❏ 1¾ cups of sugar
- ❏ spoon
- ❏ measuring cup
- ❏ small pan
- ❏ pencil
- ❏ 3 to 5 pieces of string, about 6 inches (15 cm) long
- ❏ wide-mouth pint (500 ml) jar

procedure ☆
1. Measure 1 cup of water and pour it in a small pan.
2. Have an adult heat the water on a stove until it starts to boil.
3. Remove the pan from the stove.
4. Slowly add the sugar to the water. Keep stirring the water with a spoon until all the sugar dissolves.
5. Pour the water into the jar.

Sugar

Dissolve sugar in water.

6. Cut 3 to 5 pieces of string. Each piece of string should be long enough to go from the top of the jar to halfway into the liquid.
7. Tie the string to a pencil.
8. Place the pencil on top of the jar so the strings hang into the sugar water.

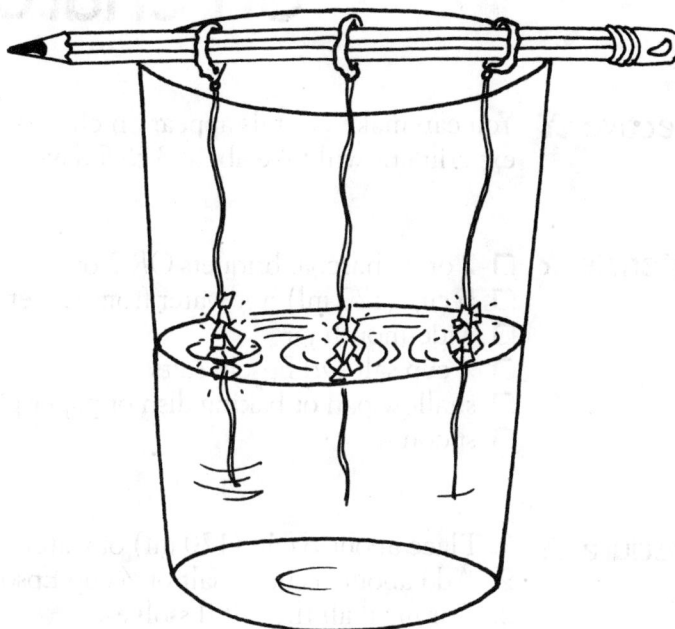

A pencil with strings.

9. Set the jar and pencil on the counter where it will not be disturbed. (It will need to stay there for about a week.) A sunny window sill is also a good place.
10. Look at the strings every day. Do you see crystals on the string? What do you think the crystals are made of?

explanation ☆ The sugar water moves up the strings. The water begins to *evaporate*, leaving only the sugar on the string. As more sugar moves onto the string, *crystals*—or, in this case, rock candy—begin to form.

After the string has many crystals on it, remove the strings and eat the rock candy you have made.

35
Growing crystals on charcoal

objective ☆ You can make crystals appear on charcoal or bricks. *Note:* This experiment will take about 3 to 5 days.

materials ☆
- ❏ 2 or 3 charcoal briquets OR 2 or 3 pieces of brick
- ❏ ½ cup (120 ml) hot water from faucet
- ❏ wide-mouth jar
- ❏ ¼ cup salt OR Epsom salts
- ❏ shallow pan or baking dish or paper plate
- ❏ spoon

procedure ☆
1. Place about ½ cup (120 ml) of water in the jar.
2. Add about ¼ cup of salt or ¼ cup Epsom salts to the hot water.
3. Stir until all the salt dissolves.
4. Soak a piece of charcoal or brick in the salt solution for about 5 minutes.
5. Remove the charcoal and place it on the plate.
6. Place the plate near a window that gets lots of sun or outside in the sun.
7. Look at the charcoal every day. Do you see crystals forming on the charcoal?

explanation ☆ When the water evaporates from the surface of the charcoal, it leaves the salt behind. If the temperature is cool, or if the air is very humid, the water will evaporate more slowly. Crystals will take longer to form.

Soak the charcoal.

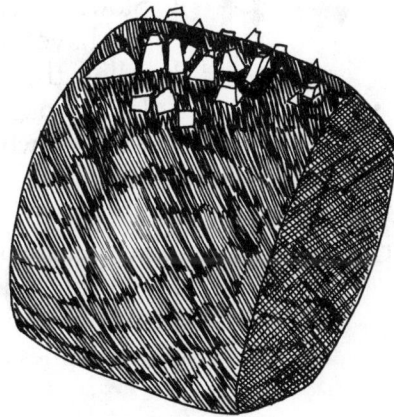

Observe the crystals on charcoal.

Try mixing two salts in the same jar before soaking the charcoal. You will probably see different kinds of crystals.

For a similar experiment, see experiment 36.

36
A crystal garden

objective ☆ You can make a crystal garden. *Note:* This experiment will take a few hours.

materials ☆
- ☐ saucepan
- ☐ spoon
- ☐ 1 cup water (from faucet)
- ☐ wide-mouth jar
- ☐ salt OR Epsom salts

procedure ☆
1. Have an adult bring 1 cup of water to boil. Lower the heat to simmer.
2. Slowly add salt or Epsom salts until no more will dissolve. You will have to add many spoonfuls of salt.
3. Allow the salt solution to cool, then pour it into a jar.
4. Drop 2 or 3 crystals of salt into the jar.
5. Observe what happens to the jar over the next few hours.

explanation ☆ More of a chemical will dissolve in hot water than in cold water. When you added a few crystals of salt to the jar, they attracted other salt molecules and pulled them out of solution. The result was that piles of salt crystals began to form.

Homemade Slime & Rubber Bones!

Crystals forming in a jar.

37
Moving colors

objective ☆ A brown color will move from one liquid to another.

materials ☆
- ❏ tall jar with lid or glass
- ❏ water from faucet
- ❏ tincture of iodine (available in drug and grocery stores)
- ❏ mineral oil (available in food and drug stores; do not use cooking oil)

procedure ☆
1. Fill the jar half-full with water.
2. Add a few drops of iodine solution to the water.
3. Put the lid on the jar and shake until the iodine is well mixed. Or stir the glass with a spoon. What color is the water?
4. Pour 1 to 2 ounces (30 to 60 ml) of mineral oil on top of the water. You should see two layers.

Color in the bottom layer.

5. Put the lid on the jar and shake again, or stir well with a spoon.
6. Observe and describe the two layers. What color is the water now? Can you explain what happened?

Color in the top layer.

explanation ☆ Mineral oil is lighter than water and, therefore, will float on top of water. Oils also do not mix well with water. Molecules of oil tend to be attracted to other molecules of oil. These facts explain why you end up with two layers. For more discussion of layers, see part 2, *Oil & floating objects.*

The iodine is more soluble in mineral oil than it is in water. *Solubility* is a measure of how much of a given compound will dissolve in a liquid. When you shook the bottle of oil and water, the oil pulled all the iodine from the water. Because the oil is lighter than water, the top layer became colored.

38
Cleaning a dirty penny

objective ☆ You can make a dirty penny shine again. *Note:* This experiment will take about 15 minutes.

materials ☆ ❏ dirty penny
❏ cup or glass
❏ lemon juice

procedure ☆ 1. Place the dirty penny in the cup.

Place a penny in a cup.

2. Pour enough lemon juice into the cup so that the penny is covered.
3. Let the penny sit in the lemon juice for 10 to 15 minutes.
4. Remove the penny. Is it still dirty?

Cover the penny with lemon juice.

explanation ☆ Pennies are made of copper. When oxygen from the air combines with copper, a new, darker compound is formed. Lemon juice contains an acid. The acid pulls the oxygen away from the copper, leaving a shiny, copper penny. For a faster way to clean the penny, see experiment 39.

39

Another way to clean a dirty penny

objective ☆ A dirty penny quickly turns shiny again. *Note:* This method is much faster than the one used in experiment 38.

materials ☆
☐ dirty penny
☐ small plate
☐ salt
☐ vinegar
☐ medicine dropper or teaspoon

procedure ☆
1. Place the penny on the plate.
2. Sprinkle salt on the penny so that the penny is covered with salt.

Cover the penny with salt.

3. Add a few drops or half of a teaspoon of vinegar to the salt-covered penny.
4. Observe how quickly the penny begins to shine.

explanation ☆ Pennies turn dark because the oxygen in the air combines with the copper in the penny, forming a new, darker chemical. Acids remove the oxygen, leaving the shiny copper.

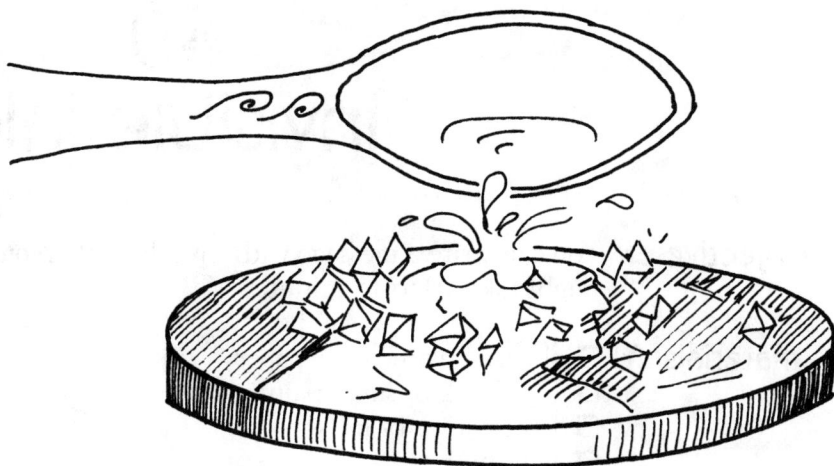

Add vinegar to the penny.

The change occurs more quickly than the change seen in experiment 38. The vinegar and the salt combine to form a much stronger acid than the acid in lemon juice. The acid formed in this experiment is the same one that is produced by your stomach.

40
Invisible ink

objective ☆ You can write a message with invisible ink. *Note:* This experiment might take 10 to 15 minutes.

materials ☆
- ❏ sheet of plain white paper
- ❏ toothpick or small paintbrush
- ❏ lemon juice or milk
- ❏ light bulb
- ❏ small bowl
- ❏ iron (optional)

procedure ☆
1. Pour some milk or lemon juice into a small bowl.
2. Dip the toothpick or paintbrush in the lemon juice or milk.

Dip a toothpick in lemon juice.

3. Use the toothpick to write on the paper. You will probably have to dip the toothpick again after every 2 or 3 letters.

Write with lemon juice.

4. Allow the message to dry.
5. Have an adult hold the paper near a light bulb that is on.
6. Do you see any writing? If you do not, have an adult use a hot iron to iron over the message on the paper.

explanation ☆ When the lemon juice or milk dries, it is colorless. The heat from the light bulb or iron causes some of the chemicals in the juice or milk to change. The new chemicals have a dark color that you can see.

Place the candle behind the bottle.

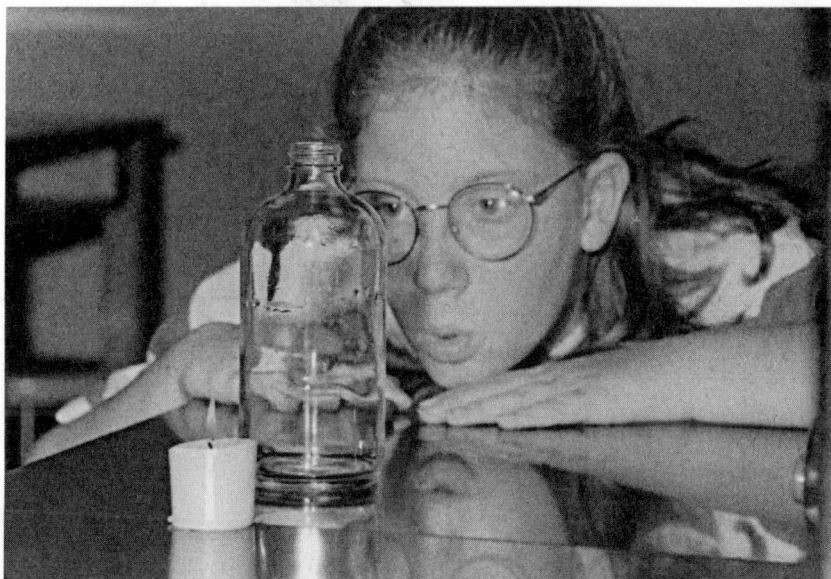

Blow at the bottle.

line. Can you explain why most trucks have curved surfaces near their roofs? For a similar experiment, see experiment 42.

Place the candle behind the book.

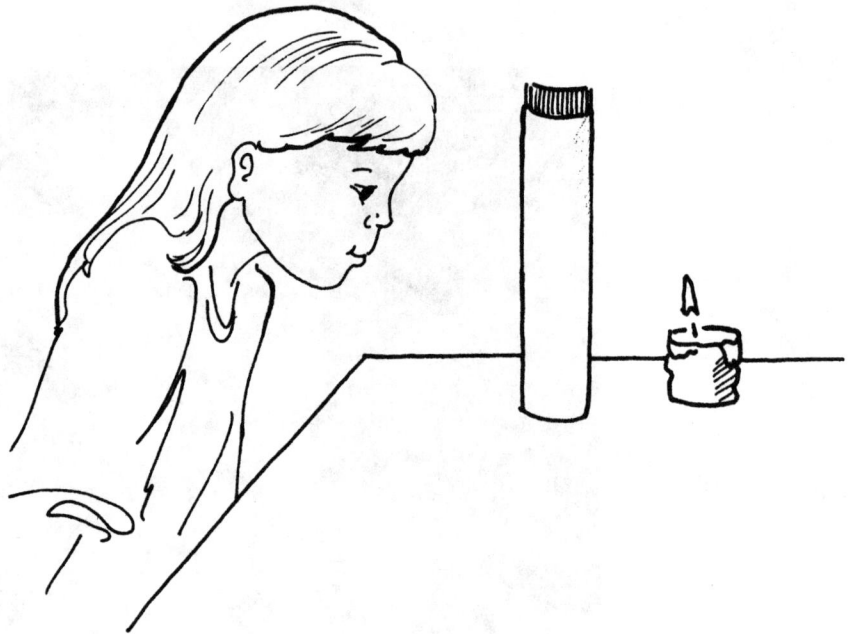

Blow at the book.

Place the candle beside the book.

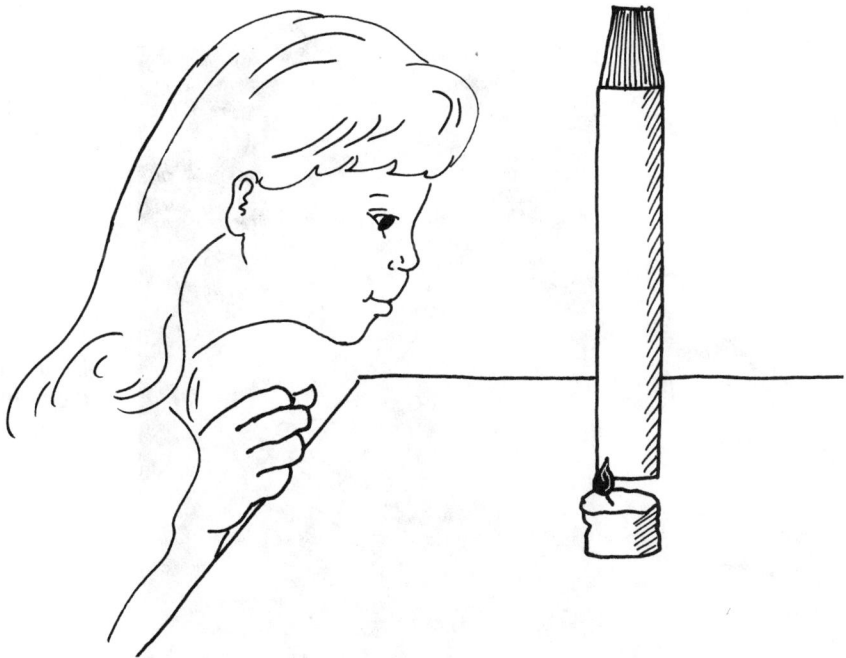

Blow at the book.

42
Using a funnel to blow out a candle

objective ☆ You will use a funnel to blow out a candle.

materials ☆ ❏ kitchen funnel
❏ candle
❏ matches

procedure ☆ 1. Place a candle on the counter.
2. Have an adult light the candle.
3. Place the narrow end of the funnel in your mouth.
4. Stand 6 to 10 inches (15 to 25 cm) away from the candle and blow. Does the candle go out?

Blow into the narrow end of the funnel.

5. If the candle does not go out, turn the funnel around. The wide mouth should be near your mouth.
6. Blow into the funnel. Does the candle now go out?

Blow into the wide end of the funnel.

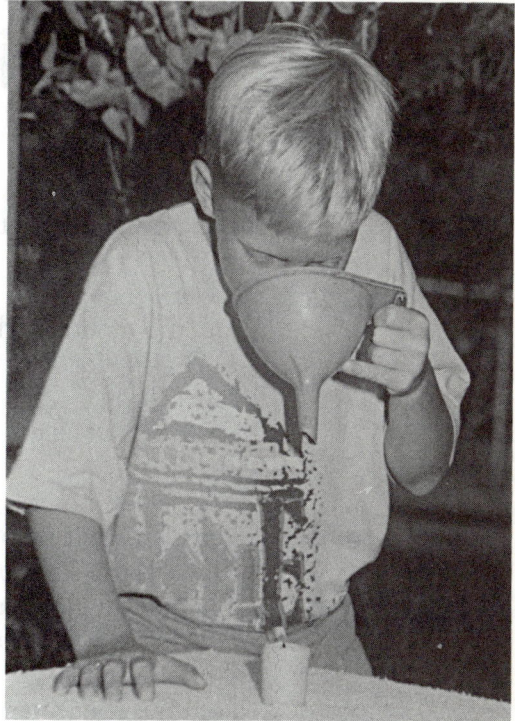

explanation ☆ When you had the narrow end in your mouth, your breath was forced out along the edges of the funnel. Very little air moved straight toward the flame. When the funnel was turned around, all the air was forced in a straight line toward the flame.

43

Sucking an egg
into a jar

objective ☆ An egg sitting on a jar will suddenly be sucked into the jar. *Note: This experiment will take about 15 minutes.*

materials ☆ ❏ 1 egg
❏ jar (the mouth of the jar should be slightly smaller than the egg)
❏ saucepan
❏ water from faucet
❏ stove

procedure ☆ 1. Have an adult prepare a hard-boiled egg. Allow the egg to cool.
2. Remove the shell of the egg.
3. Turn on the hot water and let it run until it gets hot.
4. Fill the jar with hot water and let the water stay in the jar about 2 or 3 minutes.
5. Pour out the water.
6. Place the egg on top of the jar.
7. Watch the egg. It will eventually be sucked into the jar.

explanation ☆ Hot air takes up more space than cool air. When you put the egg on the jar, the air inside the jar was hot. As the air inside the jar cooled, the air outside pushed on the egg more than did the air on the inside. The outside air forced the egg into the jar.

To get the egg out of the jar, try turning the jar upside down and blowing into the jar with a straw. This procedure might not work. You may have to break the egg into pieces to remove it from the jar.

44
Keeping water in an upside-down glass

objective ☆ When you turn a glass upside-down, the water mysteriously stays inside.

materials ☆
- ❏ glass
- ❏ index card
- ❏ water from faucet

procedure ☆
1. Hold the glass over the sink and fill it with water.
2. Place the index card on top of the glass. Be sure that the card completely covers the edges of the glass.

Place the card on top of the glass.

3. Place one hand on top of the card, and quickly turn the glass upside-down.

Turn the jar upside down.

4. Remove your hand from the card. You might have to try this experiment a few times. Does the water stay in the glass? What forces are acting on the water and the card?

explanation ☆ When you turn a glass upside-down, *gravity* pulls on the water so that water pours out of the glass. When you put the card over the glass, air is pushing on the card. In this case, air pushes up more on the card than does water pushing down. The water stays in the jar.

This experiment takes practice. You must hold the card tightly to the glass and quickly turn the glass upside-down. Do you think the water will stay in the glass if the glass is only half full? Try it and see.

Glossary

attract to move or pull toward

average a number that summarizes a group of numbers

bacteria small microscopic organisms that are found in many different places

center of gravity the point of an object that allows the entire weight to be distributed equally

charge definite quantity of electricity

circuit complete path through which electricity can move

corrugated paper paper that is shaped into folds like a fan

crystal a solid, three-dimensional shape formed from a pure chemical

curd the solid portion of milk, made up of mostly proteins

density the amount of mass in a given volume or space

displace to remove physically out of position

enzyme a specific protein that carries out a certain reaction inside a cell

evaporate to go from liquid to the vapor or gas stage

flexible easily bent

force a pushing or pulling on an object

gravity force that is responsible for things falling toward the ground; also a large force between different planets

hydrophobic water hating; things that are hydrophobic do not mix well with water

inertia tendency of an object at rest to stay at rest or of an object in motion to stay in motion

mass a measure of how much of an object is present

mineral a natural substance made up of one type of molecule

molecule smallest part of a compound that can exist by itself and still act like the compound

precipitate to come out of solution, often by combining with something else or by changing shape

reaction time how quickly a person responds to a signal or event

reflect to bounce off of one object and travel to another

repel to push or move away from

rigid stiff, not easily bent

sensor object that detects a particular kind of signal

solubility measure of how much of a given compound will dissolve in liquid

solution mixture of dissolved materials

static electricity a type of electricity that involves removing charges from one object

volume how much space something takes up

Homemade Slime & Rubber Bones!

Ind